Carol Barron, Angharad Beckett, Marieke Coussens, Annemie Desoete,
Nan Cannon Jones, Helen Lynch, Maria Prellwitz, Deborah Fenney Salkeld
Barriers to play for children and young persons with disabilities

Carol Barron, Angharad Beckett, Marieke Coussens,
Annemie Desoete, Nan Cannon Jones, Helen Lynch,
Maria Prellwitz, Deborah Fenney Salkeld

Barriers to play for children and young persons

ISBN 978-3-11-052603-5
e-ISBN (PDF) 978-3-11-052604-2
e-ISBN (EPUB) ISBN 978-3-11-052621-9

This work is licensed under the Creative Commons Attribution-NonCommercial-NoDerivs 3.0 License. For details go to http://creativecommons.org/licenses/by-nc-nd/3.0/.

© 2017 Carol Barron, Angharad Beckett, Marieke Coussens, Annemie Desoete,
Nan Cannon Jones, Helen Lynch, Maria Prellwitz, Deborah Fenney Salkeld
Published by De Gruyter Open Ltd, Warsaw/Berlin
Part of Walter de Gruyter GmbH, Berlin/Boston
The book is published with open access at www.degruyter.com.

Library of Congress Cataloging-in-Publication Data
A CIP catalog record for this book has been applied for at the Library of Congress.

www.degruyteropen.com
Cover illustration: from Abigail, aged 4 years. Abigail has Hemiparetic Cerebral Palsy.
Abgail says: "This is a picture of me playing with my big sister (Emma) in our garden".

Contents

1   Introduction —— 1
1.1   Background to the COST Action TD 1309 – Play for children with disabilities —— 2
2   **Overview of Play Studies** —— 3
2.1   Changes in children's play over time —— 4
2.2   Play, recreation and children with disabilities —— 5
3   **The Right to Play** —— 6
3.1   Critique of UNCRC in relation to children with disabilities —— 6
3.2   UN Convention on the Rights of Persons with Disabilities (CRPD) —— 7
3.3   What is a General Comment and why were they introduced? —— 8
3.4   General Comment No 9 —— 8
3.5   General Comment No 17 —— 9
3.6   International Play Association and Play for Children and Young Persons with Disabilities —— 9
4   **Definition of Disability** —— 11
4.1   How many children with disabilities are there? —— 12
4.2   Barriers to play and recreation —— 12
5   **The Home, Educational, Built and Natural Environments** —— 14
5.1   Home environment —— 14
5.2   Educational settings —— 14
5.3   The built environment —— 15
5.4   The natural environment —— 15
6   **Methodology** —— 17
7   **Findings** —— 19
7.1   Activity performance and play preferences —— 19
7.2   Physical barriers – accessibility and usability —— 20
7.3   Social barriers – attitudes and behaviours —— 23
8   **Discussion and Conclusion** —— 26
8.1   Barriers in Home, Educational, Built and Natural Settings —— 28
9   **Recommendations** —— 29
       References —— 31

Biography

Carol Barron, is a lecturer in the School of Nursing and Human Sciences at Dublin City University, Dublin, Ireland. Her professional background is in children's nursing and her academic background is in health and medical anthropology. She has extensive experience teaching within the child health field and has over 20 years' experience conducted research about children's play worlds in both urban and rural settings in the UK and Ireland and has published book chapters and journal articles in these areas as well as multiple conference presentations internationally. Dr Barron is especially interested in participatory research methodologies with children and is currently conducting folkloric archival research on children's play, games and toys. She is also working with local authorities to develop county play policies in partnership with children and young people. Dr Barron is also the Chairperson of Súgradh – the Irish national charity promoting the child's right to play and has inputted into Dublin City's Play Policy.

Angharad Beckett, is Associate Professor of Political Sociology & Deputy Director of the Centre for Disability Studies, University of Leeds, UK. The Centre for Disability Studies is an internationally renowned centre for excellence in research and teaching in this field (see: http://disability-studies.leeds.ac.uk/ or on Twitter @CDSLeeds).

She is programme leader for the Masters programmes in interdisciplinary Disability Studies and Disability Studies (Distance Learning) at the University. Her primary research interest is 'disability politics' and the struggle to build enabling and inclusive societies. She has undertaken UK Research Council (ESRC) funded research into citizenship for disabled people and disability activism and has published a book on this topic entitled 'Citizenship and Vulnerability: disability and issues of social and political engagement', published by Palgrave Macmillan.

She has also undertaken research in the area of Inclusive Education (again ESRC-funded), exploring the approaches educators use and might use to teach children and young people about disability and the need to challenge discrimination and prejudice towards disabled people. Extending her work in this area, she has recently been working in the area of Inclusive Play as part of a Leverhulme Trust-funded project in collaboration with colleagues in Engineering/Design. She is keen to explore the 'politics' of play, seeking to understand the barriers and facilitators of inclusive play for disabled children and the potential of such play for improving self-esteem amongst disabled children and encouraging positive interactions and friendships between disabled and non-disabled children.

Contact: A.E.Beckett@leeds.ac.uk

Marieke Coussens, is master in Occupational Therapy with expertise in working with young children and their parents with developmental disabilities.

She is junior researcher (PhD student) and Ghent University and a teacher at the Artevelde University college (occupational therapists)

At Ghent University she is attached to the research group Learning Disabilities of the Department of Experimental-Clinical and Health Psychology Developmental Disorders and to the faculty of Medicine (Rehabilitation Science). The research group Developmental Disorders and association research group Learning Disabilities of Ghent University have extensive experience in research in early characteristics of learning disabilities. In addition she is conducting research on participation (as defined by the ICF-CY) of young children with Attention Deficit disorders, Autism and Developmental Coordination disorders. She is also a clinician working with these young children and their parents.

At Artevelde University college she is promotor of the research and advice center 'Learn+' where studies on atypical learning are coordinated with an interdisciplinary approach.

Annemie Desoete, is master in education with expertise in learning disabilities (especially dyscaculia and dyslexia).

She is senior researcher (full professor) and Ghent University and at the Artevelde University college (speech therapists)

At Ghent University she is attached to the research group Learning Disabilities of the Department of Experimental-Clinical and Health Psychology Developmental Disorders.

The research group Developmental Disorders and association research group Learning Disabilities of Ghent University have extensive experience in research in early characteristics of learning disabilities. In addition she is conducting research on serious gaming, metacognition; executive functioning, time related problems and the learning of fractions in children with learning disabilities. She is also promoter of PhD studies on ASD and on number sense in young children.

At Artevelde University college she is head promotor of the research and advice center 'Learn+' where studies on atypical learning are coordinated with an interdisciplinary approach.

More information : http://www.ekgp.ugent.be/index.php?position=5x1x0&page=ADES
https://biblio.ugent.be/person/801001505476

She was the promotor or copromotor of 14 PhDstudies.

Currently she is promotor of

- PhD Elke Baten The role of motivation, communication, self-compassion and well-being in (a)typical numerical skills – since 1.10.2015
- PhD Ehud Fries 'the influence of software on accelerating reading/math abilities for children with learning difficulties in Hebrew' since 18.11.2014

 **Nan Cannon Jones**, During my teaching career I have worked in mainstream infant/junior schools, in specialist provisions, from birth to 5 years, and as an advisory teacher for children aged 5 to 18 years. Firstly for Children with an Autism Spectrum Condition and latterly for children with a Physical and Neurological Impairment.

I studied for a Certificate in Education, for Infant and Junior Children at Hockerill College and for a Master's Degree in Special Education at the University of Birmingham. My studies, at university, focussed on Children with Autism and my Action Research project explored sensory perceptual issues for pre-school children with Autism Spectrum Conditions. The research was part of regular and routine activities already established in a pre-school specialist provision for children with a range of disabilities. The research was carried out through working in close partnership with parents, carers and other involved professionals.

My research enquiry analysed the reactions and responses of pre-school children to environmental stimulation. The enquiry indicated that practitioners need to focus on the sensory abilities of children with autism rather than their sensory difficulties. The results showed that children with autism do sense the world in the same way as those following a typical pattern of development but that their reactions and responses are not always seen to be purposeful. With this research in mind sensitively structured play routines were developed to help children to make sense of and give meaning to everyday experiences.

As an independent specialist, I plan and deliver parent workshops and staff training, based on the National Autistic Societies SPELL framework and have also planned and written a series of workshops for a National Charity. At present my independent outreach work involves supporting parents, Early Years settings, after school clubs and church groups.

I have been included in and supported a research project with Hertfordshire University developing the use of KASPAR, a childlike humanoid robot, to develop Social Interaction and Social Communication for children with autism through collaborative play. Interactions with others can be unpredictable and frightening, KASPAR acts as mediator for the children who first, with adult support, interact and play with the robot, this happens initially on a 1:1 basis until the children are ready to play with KASPAR in a small group (2/3 children).

As part of this project I designed an assessment document that fits with both the Early Years Foundation Stage (http://www.foundationyears.org.uk) and the World Health Organisation International Classification of Functioning, Disability and Health (ICF WHO 2001) document. This has been well received by a range of local professionals.

I am delighted to be a member of the Ludi research project investigating play for children with disabilities.

Helen Lynch, is an Occupational Therapist and an Occupational Scientist who has worked to enable children participate in the world through engaging in occupation, especially play. Helen worked as an occupational therapist for 20 years with families and children with special needs in many different services in Ireland: for children with cognitive, sensory and physical disabilities. She, specialised in environmental access, sensory integration, and occupational development and service development. Since 2003, she has focused her work on research and teaching. She joined the Department of Occupational Science and Occupational Therapy in University College Cork as full-time lecturer and Director of Brookfield Clinic and of the graduate studies programme in the department. She teaches modules related to children, research and service delivery and effectiveness, and supervises student research for undergraduate, and postgraduate students related to children and family-centred practice.

Helen gained a Diploma in Montessori Education and completed a master's degree researching time-use (occupation and environments) of children in middle-childhood (2007). In 2012, she completed a PhD in social sciences exploring physical play environments in the homes of infants under two. Her research has continued to focus in particular on play and early childhood, including home, community and school playspaces. Using inclusive approaches in research, Helen has worked with children to design their outdoor play spaces, to inform us about play and play occupation, and has worked to enable play through design and the development of tools to support practitioners. Through this work so far, there is support for the need for further work in identifying children's play occupations that are culturally and contextually relevant. In turn this will inform practitioners when using play-based approaches in early intervention for children with disabilities and will also strengthen family-centred practices. We have a lot to learn from the children and families we work with!

Maria Prellwitz, is a senior lecturer with a PhD in Occupational Therapy at Luleå University of Technology, Sweden. In 1999 she joined the division of Occupational Therapy as full-time lecturer. Maria co-ordinates the Occupational Therapy program third year, focusing on teaching scientific research methods. Her other main area of teaching is within pediatrics. She supervises several undergraduate research projects mainly related to children and accessibility issues.

Maria's main research focus is to elucidate the children's own voices on different issues. Her current research has a focus on: Play for children with disabilities and accessibility and usability of different environments for children with different abilities. Her main focus has been on playgrounds. Another focus is to elucidate children with disabilities experiences of play within their rehabilitation.

She is also involved in a research project together with the department of civil engineering regarding a laser navigator that complements the white cane and helps persons with visual impairment to orientate. This is a unique solution to how persons with visual impairment can find and experience direction and distance to objects in the environment. She also runs several projects regarding the development of e-learning at the University.

Currently Maria is Vice-chairman of the board of the faculty of humanities and social sciences and Associate Dean of the faculty of arts and social sciences.

Deborah Fenney Salkeld, I completed my PhD exploring disabled people's access to sustainable lifestyles at the University of Leeds in 2015, in the School of Sociology and Social Policy. My broad research interests are disability equality and sustainability, as well as related issues of policy and activism. As access to the natural environment is a significant part of access to sustainable lifestyles, however, this is also a particular interest. I currently work in the healthcare sector.

1 Introduction

The work of the LUDI network, established and funded by COST in 2014, is underpinned by a commitment to the right of children and young persons with disabilities to recreation and play, as stated in international Conventions on the Rights of the Child and Rights of Persons with Disabilities. These human rights conventions place signatories under an obligation to put in place an appropriate set of entitlements, actions and resources to ensure their implementation. Importantly, the LUDI network recognises the importance of play and recreation for children with disabilities *in* and *of* itself – that is, play *for its own sake* – and its centrality to children and young people's overall well-being and quality of life. Play and recreation is more than an enabler or a tool in relation to social, educational, physical and psychological development and health promotion/maintenance. Play has intrinsic value to all children.

This book examines the environmental barriers to play and recreation in everyday worlds of children and young persons with disabilities as identified within current literature. We commence with a brief overview of the work of the LUDI network, a COST TD Action TD1309 project, to provide context. We then provide a brief overview of the interdisciplinary nature of play studies (Henricks, 2008). We consider how play has changed in recent decades and what is known about play and recreation for children and young persons with disabilities. This is followed by a closer examination of the Convention of the Rights of the Child (1989), Convention of the Rights of Persons with Disabilities (2008) and General Comments 9 (2007) and 17 (2013) as they relate to play and recreation for children and young persons with disabilities. Since disability is a contested concept, we next outline our definition of disability and justify our use of the International Classification of Function, Disability and Health (ICF; WHO, 2002), International Classification of Function, Disability and Health-Children and Youth (ICF-CY; WHO, 2007) and associated terminology. Finally, we provide a detailed narrative review of existing research and knowledge surrounding play for children with disabilities within four key locations/spaces.

Play and recreation does not occur in a 'vacuum' (Meires, 2007); it happens 'somewhere' in a physical, social and cultural setting (Barron, 2013). The locations where children with disabilities engage in play and the influences on their choice of location and activity have only recently begun to be explored, and there is need for further research in this area. Children of course play wherever they are (NCB, 2002). Reading across literature in Children's and Childhood Studies and the reports by organisations such as the National Children's Bureau (UK) and Play England, four key locations for play, each broadly defined, can nevertheless be identified as important venues for children's play: the home, educational settings, the built environment and the natural environment. In this book, we focus on each of these locations in turn, considering the unique and the generic barriers in operation. We conclude with a discussion of the findings of our literature review and make recommendations for future research and policy work in this area.

1.1 Background to the COST Action TD 1309 – Play for children with disabilities

This Action aims at the creation of a novel and autonomous field of research and intervention on play for children with disabilities. The network has three main objectives:

  a. Collecting and systematising all existing competence and skills: educational researches, clinical initiatives, know-how of resource centres and users' associations
  b. Developing new knowledge related to settings, tools and methodologies associated with the play of children with disabilities
  c. Disseminating the best practices emerging from the joint effort of researchers, practitioners and users

Play for children with disabilities is the object of a fragmented set of studies, and it has given rise, in different countries and at different times, to niche projects (i.e. social robotics for autistic children, adapted toys for children with cognitive and motor disabilities, accessible playground areas). There is a need, however, for transdisciplinary cooperation between researchers and practitioners in the fields of psycho-pedagogical sciences, social sciences, health and rehabilitation sciences, humanities, assistive technologies and robotics, together with the vital contribution of children with disabilities, their families and friends and support organisations to find ways to ensure and empower children's right to play.

The main objective of the Action, therefore, is to spread awareness of the importance of giving children with disabilities the opportunity to play, while ensuring equity in their exercise of the right to play and by putting play at the centre of multidisciplinary research and innovation in relation to the lives and well-being of children with disabilities. Within this Action, there are four working groups. Each has specific objectives. The objective of Working Group 3 – to which the authors of this book are associated – is to examine the impact of environmental factors on play for children with disabilities. Environmental factors are understood here in terms of WHO's International Classification of Functioning, Disability and Health (ICF). Such factors include products and technologies, services, systems, laws and policies, the natural environment and human-made changes to the environment, support, relationships and attitudes (both individual and societal). These factors may operate as barriers or facilitators of play for children with disabilities.

In this book, arising from LUDI Working Group 3, we explore the environmental factors operating as *barriers*. Identifying and understanding these barriers is a vital first step in the process of their removal.

2 Overview of Play Studies

> When it comes to making theoretical statements about what play is, there is little agreement among us and much ambiguity (Sutton-Smith, 1997: 1).

Almost two decades ago, Brian Sutton-Smith, a leading international researcher and theorist on the topic of children's play, famously articulated what many professional disciplines and researchers already intuitively knew. Play is something we all recognise when we see it, yet it defies a universally agreed definition. Play studies do not constitute an academic discipline but rather an interdiscipline or multidiscipline (Henricks, 2008). Brian Sutton-Smith in his 1997 text *The Ambiguity of Play* reviewed and clustered hundreds of play studies into seven distinct play 'rhetorics' or discourses. These rhetorics, he argued, operate as cultural perspectives or lenses that encourage us to focus on certain kinds of play and discourage other forms of inquiry.

A 'play as progress' rhetoric was the overwhelming dominant discourse of the 20th century. Advocates of this approach believe that children adapt and develop through their play. This belief in play as progress is held in high esteem by most Western cultures. According to Sutton-Smith (1997), however, its relevance to play has been assumed rather than demonstrated.

Most prominent among the contributors to the rhetoric of play as progress are play studies from psychology, developmental studies (Piaget, 1945) and education (Kaplan, 2008). Psychologists have focused on the actions, orientations and experiences of individual children (Henricks, 2008). Their principal concern has been human learning or socialisation rather than play itself. Educational academics, specifically those focusing on early childhood, have been great supporters of the more idealised forms of play (Dockett and Perry, 2005; Einarsdottir, 2005) and view particular types of play as a medium to help children learn and acquire more knowledge. Much of the discourse from children's geographies published within the last two decade also reflects a play as progress rhetoric, focusing on how children's development is advanced or curtailed by their use of space (Aitken, 2001; Valentine and Holloway, 2000). Health-related disciplines, during the same time period, have maintained a strong focus on physical activity play as having an important role in preventing childhood obesity (Peirson et al., 2015).

Importantly, Sutton-Smith (1997, pp. 42) suggests that this 'rhetoric' is not unproblematic: 'the progress rhetoric appears to serve adult needs rather than the needs of children' by facilitating adults' intervention and manipulation of children's play worlds. Within interdisciplinary disability studies, this critique has been developed by Goodley and Runswick-Cole (2010), who describe how children with disabilities, together with all children, are likely to be subject to activities that masquerade as play, but are really vehicles for education, development 'attainment' and so forth, but are also more likely to be considered 'deficient' in the abilities necessary for play and, consequently, to be subject to even greater adult intervention and surveillance in their play activities.

The LUDI network is conscious of this need to liberate play for children with disabilities from the worst excesses or 'applications' of the play-as-progress rhetoric while acknowledging that play can and does promotes child development, health, well-being and other positive 'outcomes' for all children. Nevertheless, any denial of the right to play for children with disabilities is a denial of their right to experience the many benefits of play. Where the 'play-as-progress' rhetoric becomes too dominant, there is a risk of the child's right to play for the sake of play, for recreation, diversion or pleasure, being in effect denied or undervalued. Hence, the LUDI network has adopted a particular definition of play from the study by Garvey (1990). Accordingly, the network views play as a range of voluntary, intrinsically motivated activities normally associated with recreational pleasure and enjoyment (Garvey, 1990). This definition can include all kinds of activities performed with ludic intention (i.e. playful behaviour) and moves away from the narrower but dominant 'play-as-progress' rhetoric.

2.1 Changes in children's play over time

Over the past one and a half centuries, there has been a gradual long-term shift in many countries in the 'spaces of childhood', from outdoors to indoors, from woods, fields and streets, to back and front gardens, bedrooms and commercial and other formal play sites (Burke, 2005). There has also been a shift in playmates, from family members, including siblings and cousins, to the peer group, as well as an increase in small group and solitary play, with geographical proximity no longer the predominant way that play groups are formed. At the same time, there has been a shift in the material culture of childhood, as improvised items and toys sold to parents to impart useful skills gave way to fantasy toys marketed directly to children (Mintz, 2009).

The most significant trends have been a decline in intergenerational amusements and an increase in sedentary, isolated play (Sutton-Smith, 1997) and electronically mediated play (Henricks, 2015; Kline, 2004) and a decline in wholly unsupervised, free, unstructured play (Meire, 2007). But these trends have developed more slowly and incrementally than many assume (Mintz, 2009), and their roots lie, largely, in demographic developments, not in misplaced cultural values. Similar to all cultures, children's culture itself is not static. In every historical era, diverse children's cultures co-exist, varying according to children's developmental stage, ability or disability, age, class, ethnicity, gender, location and race.

2.2 Play, recreation and children with disabilities

Despite decades of research on play, recreation and childhood for children in general, few studies have focused specifically on free play for children and young persons with disabilities. Existing studies have found that children with disabilities experience significantly reduced participation in play and leisure in general and are at risk for health and social difficulties as a result (King et al., 2009). Children with disabilities are often excluded from outdoor play due to multiple factors such as functional abilities (impairment), physical inaccessibility, attitudinal barriers and poor social supports (Anaby, Law and Tepicky, 2013; Tonkin et al., 2014). In a scoping review of research that examined the patterns of participation in activities outside of formal school, Tonkin et al. (2014) found that taking part in everyday activities for children with disabilities, such as play and recreation, is vital to a sense of belonging within the community, and a modified environment can facilitate this (McManus et al., 2008; Tonkin et al., 2014).

Many studies have found that children and young persons with disabilities take part in fewer activities as their same age peers, yet they enjoy similar activities (Engel-Yeger et al., 2009; Hilton et al., 2008; Imms et al., 2008; Law et al., 2013). Differences exist with whom, and where, children and young persons with disabilities take part in play and recreation as well as organised sports; for example, they participate more with their families (King et al., 2010; Kraemer et al., 1997) and closer to home (Imms et al., 2008; Majnemer et al., 2008). The 'tether length' (Barron, 2013) or geographical distance from the home for children with disabilities would appear to be ever more restricted in comparison to their similar-aged, non-disabled peers. In one of the few studies seeking children and young people's views, Heah et al. (2007) interviewed children with physical and neurological disabilities and their parents. They found that children participate in the activities that they find fun and liked a feeling of success (in their play), interacting with others and also doing activities themselves (Heah et al., 2007). This confirms the value of play in these children's lives.

3 The Right to Play

From an international legal perspective, the right of all children to play can be traced back to the proclamation in the 1959 Declaration of the Rights of the Child, which marks the first major international consensus on the fundamental principles of children's rights: 'The child shall have full opportunity for play and recreation [...] society and the public authorities shall endeavor to promote the enjoyment of this right' (Principle. 7). This proclamation was reinforced in the Convention on the Rights of the Child 1989 (UNCRC), which explicitly states in Article 31 that:

> States Parties recognize the right of the child to rest and leisure, to engage in play and recreational activities appropriate to the age of the child and to participate freely in cultural life and the arts.

The UNCRC has been ratified by 192 of 196 countries, including all European countries. Of the 54 articles in this convention, Article 31 is highly significant as it represents the first time that the international community has recognised the importance of play and recreation in the lives of children and young people. Play is now a human right enshrined in international law.

Two other articles under the UNCRC also make specific reference to children and young persons with disabilities: Article 2 outlines the principle of non-discrimination and includes disability as grounds for protection from discrimination and Article 23 highlights the special efforts that States Parties must make to realise these rights. Article 12 of the Convention is also of note for this work as it focuses on the child and young person's right to express their opinion and have it taken into account in any matter or procedure affecting them.

> States Parties shall assure to the child who is capable of forming his or her own views the right to express those views freely in all matters affecting the child, the views of the child being given due weight in accordance with the age and maturity of the child. (United Nations High Commissioner for Human Rights 1989)

For the first time, we have an international agreement that states that all children and young people have the right to express their views and have them taken into account (Morrow and Richards, 1996).

3.1 Critique of UNCRC in relation to children with disabilities

At a legislative level, the UNCRC is based on the premise that children are equal to adults and should be seen as 'persons'. International policies are increasingly constructing children as rights-bearing citizens rather than immature beings. There is no universal agreement on this view, however, and Jean La Fontaine (1997) argues that whatever the rhetoric, at a legislative level, many in the West still reject the idea of children as persons. The UNCRC also has at its core a universalised view of 'the child' based on Western assumptions about children's 'best interests' (Bluebond-Langer and Korbin, 2007) and a single standard of age which is 18 years and under. This universal definition of children is problematic as it assumes that all children and childhoods are the same globally irrespective of culture, gender, ethnicity, history or disability, despite evidence to the contrary (LeVine, 2007).

When this dominant discourse of childhood is integrated as a normative baseline into human rights discourse, it enforces views of 'other' childhoods as abnormal and problematic. Thus, children and young persons with disabilities can be viewed as 'other' and therefore problematic. Despite the limitations of the convention, however, non-ratification of the UNCRC by a state would signal their failure to recognise all children's rights broadly. Thus, the UNCRC may be regarded as a milestone in how we view children and childhood in terms of both the development of national and international policies related to children and young people and the encouragement of scholarly activity that includes the views and active participation of all children and acknowledges the importance of play.

3.2 UN Convention on the Rights of Persons with Disabilities (CRPD)

The Convention on the Rights of Persons with Disabilities (CRPD) was adopted by the United Nations General Assembly in 2006 and came into force in 2008. To date, eight European countries have yet to ratify this convention fully. The CRPD builds on the Standard Rules on the Equalization of Opportunities for Persons with Disabilities (1994) and World Program of Action on Disabled Persons (1982), neither of which are legally binding treaties. The purposes of the CRPD are to promote and protect the enjoyment of all human rights and fundamental freedoms by all persons with disabilities and to promote respect for their inherent dignity. The CRPD marks a 'paradigm shift' (Harpur, 2012) in attitudes and approaches to persons with disabilities and is a move away from an approach where persons with disabilities are considered objects of interventions, to an acknowledgement of them as subjects of human rights, able to make decisions about their lives and futures and as claimants of rights on their own behalf.

The CRPD has created a vigorous new disability rights model that empowers disabled people's organisations and creates a new paradigm for disability scholars (Harpur, 2012). Article 7 of the CRPD places a clear obligation on governments to ensure that children with disabilities enjoy all human rights on an equal basis with other children (CRPD, 2008). It further stipulates that:

> States Parties shall ensure that children with disabilities have the right to express their views freely on all matters affecting them, their views being given due weight in accordance with their age and maturity, on an equal basis with other children, and to be provided with disability and age-appropriate assistance to realize that right. (CRPD 2008, pp. 10).

These core principles, also enshrined and monitored by the UNCRC, constitute an important legacy for the fulfilment of the rights of children with disabilities and their full participation in society. Article 30 of the CRPD promotes the full and effective participation and inclusion in society of children and young people with disabilities, as well as adults with disabilities, and focuses specifically on access issues:

> To ensure that children with disabilities have equal access with other children to participation in play, recreation and leisure and sporting activities, including those activities in the school system. (CRPD, 2008, pp. 22)

Article 30 focuses on equal access issues for children and young persons with disabilities to participate in play and recreation, thereby acknowledging an existing concern that children and young people with disabilities experience barriers in relation to access for play and recreation. The challenge following the ratification of the CRPD, however, is how to ensure the CRPD is implemented as a roadmap for change and not just as a technical standard (Harpur, 2012).

3.3 What is a General Comment and why were they introduced?

General Comments are developed over time to help States interpret articles within a convention as a part of a monitoring and feedback program following ratification of Conventions. To date, 17 General Comments have been developed related to the UNCRC, and of those, two have specific significance to play and children with disabilities: General Comment no 9 (children with disabilities) and General Comment no 17 (right to play and leisure).

3.4 General Comment No 9

The General Comment on children with disabilities was prepared and published in 2007 as a response to feedback from States that children were still experiencing serious difficulties in having their rights protected. This was evident through multiple factors including societal, cultural, attitudinal and physical barriers and related in particular to discrimination and exclusion from leading a full life (Articles 2 and 23 of UNCRC). In particular, the comment states:

> The attainment of full inclusion of children with disabilities in the society is realised when children are given the opportunity, places and time to play with each other (children with disabilities and no disabilities). Training for recreation, leisure and play should be included for school-aged children with disabilities. (General Comment No 9, pp. 70)

3.5 General Comment No 17

In the 26 years since the launch of the UNCRC on the rights of the child, the developed world in particular has seen significant increases in urban populations (Marshall, 2007), 'stranger danger' fears (Valentine and Holloway, 2000), increased commercial play spaces and play provision internationally (McKendrick et al. 2000), which all influence the ways children and young people engage in recreation.

This is compounded globally by specific demands such as increasing educational demands, domestic work and child labour (Edmonds and Pavcnik, 2005), which all diminish the time available for children to enjoy their rights as outlined in Article 31. General Comment 17 was developed to address these concerns specifically and reflects the committee's specific concerns about the difficulties faced by particular categories of children in relation to achieving equality vis-a-vis the rights defined in Article 31. Children and young persons with disabilities are clearly and consistently identified within General Comment 17 as a specific group who have difficulties ensuring that their human rights related to play and recreation are met.

3.6 International Play Association and Play for Children and Young Persons with Disabilities

Numerous international play organisations and associations lobbied for General Comment 17, among them being the International Play Association (IPA), an international non-governmental organisation whose purpose is to protect, preserve and promote the child's right to play as a fundamental human right. In May 2015, the IPA issued a position paper *on The Play Rights of Children with Disabilities* in response to international concerns on the part of their members about the multiple barriers that children with disabilities may face in exercising their right to play:

> Disabled children have the same right as other children to sufficient time and space to play freely, in the ways they choose, without being unduly overprotected. Many disabled children face multiple barriers that restrict their day-to-day opportunities to play. These barriers include the imposition of activities determined by adults, inaccessible facilities and environments, negative attitudes and inappropriate social policies and programs which restrict the lives of disabled children. IPA believes that families, care-givers, professionals and authorities must recognize the value of play, both as a right in itself and a means of achieving optimum development. Every child is different. To enable each child to enjoy their right to play, pro-active measures are needed to remove disabling barriers and promote accessibility. (The Play Rights of Children with Disabilities. IPA Position Paper 2015)

The focus on 'time and space', and play chosen by the child, echoes the views expressed in General Comment 17 and indeed was one of the rationales for its development. The acknowledgement that children can be 'unduly overprotected' mirrors much of the rhetoric of the last decade of risk-averse societies and cultures where the unrealistic goal appears to be *'risk-free environments'* for children to engage in play (Barron, 2014; Livingstone, 2002). The points highlighted by the IPA are not unique to children with disabilities; rather they are affecting the play worlds of all children.

4 Definition of Disability

Understandings of disability have evolved considerably over time. The traditional medical model views disability as a feature of the person directly caused by injury or disease, congenital or acquired and as a problem requiring medical or other intervention. The focus of this model is cure and/or care, and it is associated with approaches that seek to 'fix' the minds/bodies of individuals. In contrast, the social model of disability views disability as a socially created problem that can only be solved through societal solutions – by the removal of disabling barriers (be they physical, economic, political, social, cultural and so on). From this perspective, focusing on a person's impairment or difference solely, or predominantly, is problematic. This approach demands a societal response, since the problem is created by an un-accommodating physical, cultural, social and economic environment that is structured around the needs of a mythical able-bodied population.

The ICF (2002) and the ICF-CY (2007) were developed to classify health characteristics based on an integrated view of health and well-being. The model of disability supported by the ICF is the biopsychosocial model, which is an integration of these approaches (individual/medical and social models): *biological, psychological and social*. The ICF is the WHO framework for classification of health and disability at both individual and population levels and is officially endorsed by all 191 WHO Member States as the international standard to describe and measure health and disability. The ICF model is represented diagrammatically in Figure 4.1. This diagram demonstrates how the ICF includes constructs that capture functioning (impairment) and disability.

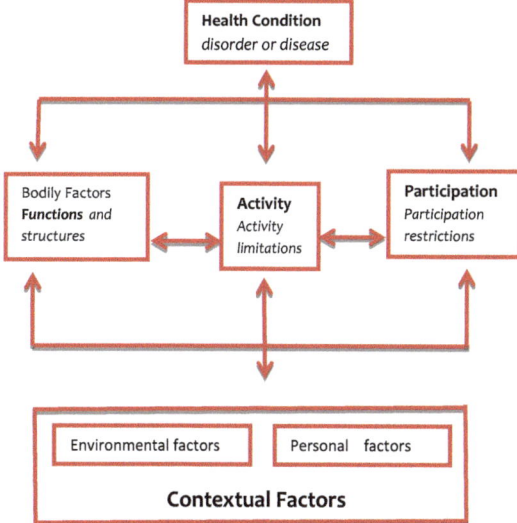

Figure 4.1. The ICF – CY Model including constructs capturing functioning and disability. Adapted from Simeonsson (2009) and WHO (2007)

The ICF (2002) model clearly acknowledges that 'on their own, neither a social nor medical model is adequate, although both are partially valid' (WHO 2002, pp.9). The ICF recognises that disability is a complex phenomenon denoting the negative aspects of the interaction between an individual (with a health condition) and contextual factors. Thus, this is a relational concept of disability.

4.1 How many children with disabilities are there?

The WHO and the World Bank estimate that there are more than a billion persons with disabilities worldwide (WHO, 2012). This is approximately 15% of the world's population. Estimates of the prevalence of children and young persons with disabilities vary significantly, depending on the definition and measures used. Currently, there are no reliable and representative estimates based on actual measurement of the number of children and young persons with disabilities (Maulik and Darmstadt, 2007; WHO, 2011). Furthermore, the limitations of census and general household surveys to capture childhood disability and the absence of registries in many developing countries contribute to lower estimates (UNICEF, 2008).

The Global Burden of Disease (2008) estimates the number of children and young people aged 0–14 years experiencing 'moderate or severe disability' to be 93 million (5.1%), with 13 million (0.7%) children experiencing severe difficulties (2008). UNICEF (2005/6) estimated the number of children with disabilities younger than 18 years to be 150 million. A review of the literature from developing countries reports child disability prevalence from 0.4% to 12.7% depending on the study and assessment tool (Maulik and Darmstadt, 2007). Many of the problems in identifying and characterising disability are a result of the absence of cultural and language-specific tools for assessment (Hartley and Newton, 2009). This latter point may account, in part, for the variation in prevalence figures and suggests that children with disabilities are not being identified or receiving the services that they need, globally.

4.2 Barriers to play and recreation

> *Multiple barriers* impede access by children with disabilities to the rights provided for in Article 31, including exclusion from school, informal and social arenas where friendships are formed and where play and recreation take place, isolation at the home, cultural attitudes and negative stereotypes which are hostile to and rejecting of children with disabilities, physical inaccessibility [......] policies that exclude [......] communication barriers [......] *Pro-active measures are needed to remove barriers and promote accessibility to and availability of inclusive opportunities for children with disabilities to participate in all these activities* (General Comment 17. 50, pp.16).

General Comments 17 and 9 clearly acknowledge the 'multiple barriers' faced by children with disabilities to engage in a meaningful way in self-selected play and recreation in physical spaces of their choice. Therefore, we have formatted the following section of this book to examine the available published literature that focuses on play with children with disabilities under four main locations or play spaces: the home, the school, the built environment and the natural environment. While acknowledging that these terms/physical spaces are not mutually exclusive, we provide broad definitions of each to focus the discussion.

5 The Home, Educational, Built and Natural Environments

5.1 Home environment

The term 'home' has many multilayered and multifaceted dimensions, which make it difficult to define explicitly or describe objectively (Benjamin, 1995; Moore, 2000; Rapoport, 1995). A sophisticated collection of literature focusing on the meaning of home exists across academic disciplines. Within this literature, there is a certain consistency in core ideas. For example, terms such as privacy, security, family, intimacy, comfort and control dominate most definitions of 'home' (Putnam and Newton, 1990). In addition, recurrent meanings for home such as a place of retreat, safety, relaxation, self-expression, continuity, freedom, independence, social status, refuge, permanence, ownership, financial asset and self-identity indicate that both empirical and theoretical research are talking about the same construct (Allen, 2008; Somerville, 1997). The home can be a concrete physical object and an abstract term reflecting an individual's relationship with that object and can consist of multiple diverse situations or permutations of 'home' (Nilsen and Rogers, 2005). In its everyday usage, the term 'home' can be used to describe many types of environments in multiple geographic locations and scale but does not discriminate or distinguish between them. For children with disabilities, home may include temporary care settings such as hospitals and institutions or long-term settings such as orphanages.

5.2 Educational settings

Within this book, the term 'educational settings' is defined as any setting where one can receive an educational experience such as kindergarten, primary and secondary schools. Educational settings can be formal or informal such as school playgrounds, after-school-clubs and so forth. Both formal and informal educational settings should provide a safe learning environment in which children's developmental needs can be met and in which active learning can take place (Moyles, 2013). Furthermore, formal and informal educational settings are places or spaces enabling children to make links between their internal being and external reality, make relationships with others, learn to discriminate and make judgments, investigate and create and imagine and formulate ideas. Thus, the home is also the dominant non-formal educational setting in which learning and child development needs are met. It must also be acknowledged that within educational settings, children are all unique, and some children with and without disabilities need more 'playfulness' and 'action' than others.

5.3 The built environment

Within this book, the term 'built environment' is viewed as that part of the physical environment that is constructed by human activity (Saelens and Handy, 2008). Urban planners use an assortment of terminologies when defining aspects of the built environment, which may appear interchangeable; however, the distinctions among these are important. 'Urban design' usually refers to the design of cities and the physical elements within them and is concerned with the function and appeal of public spaces such as parks. 'Land use' typically refers to the distribution of activities across space, including the location and density of different activities, such as residential, commercial, industrial and other activities. The 'transportation system' includes the physical infrastructure of roads, sidewalks, bike paths, railroad tracks, bridges and so forth.

Thus, the built environment comprises urban design, land use, the transportation system and encompasses multiple patterns of human activity within the physical environment (Handy et al., 2002). A core concept for evaluating social inclusion and the built environment is that of universal design, also known as building-for-all or barrier-free design (Iwarsson and Stahl, 2003). This concept includes two core aspects: accessibility and usability. Accessibility can be defined as the ability of a person to utilise the design features of the environment, for example, to use a slope rather than steps. Accessibility also refers to compliance with standard guidelines for accessible environments. Usability refers to the ability of a person to access and use the environment on equal terms with others: it relates to function (see also ISO 2008 for helpful definitions of these concepts). Both accessibility and usability are vitally important.

Within the built environment, children's neighbourhood places are considered to be 'community open spaces and communal facilities in a neighborhood that children consider as being especially important to them in terms of psychological, behavioral, and symbolic meaning' (Min and Lee, 2006, pp. 51). In relation to built environments and play, specific contexts, therefore, include playgrounds, parks and neighbourhood play spaces.

5.4 The natural environment

Any definition of the term 'natural environment' is dependent on context rather than a set definition. For the purpose of this work, the term 'natural environment' comprises all living and non-living things that occur naturally. It also includes a continuum of human–environment influence, ranging from total human-designed space to 'pure' wilderness (Carver et al., 2002). Natural environments have been defined as 'environments not designed or cultivated by humans' (Fjørtoft 2004, p24). Today, however, most natural environments that children encounter are the product of interaction between nature and humans, for example, suburban gardens (Tuan, 1978). Thus, in an urban context, a child may have daily access to a range of natural spaces with varying degrees of human design and modifications (Lester and Maudsley, 2007).

6 Methodology

Our approach is that of a literature review. We provide the reader with an overview of what is known about barriers to play for children with disabilities in these four key contexts. By exploring knowledge to date, we map the territory for further research in this area. The relative merits of narrative versus systematic reviews are much debated. Critics of narrative reviews suggest that they lack objectivity and transparency. They argue that systematic reviews are more rigorous, objective and transparent. Systematic reviews can, however, be difficult to undertake by large teams of researchers, and with mindful of these difficulties, we chose not to adopt this approach or, rather, not to make any claim to have conducted such a review. We strove, however, to mitigate certain criticisms directed towards traditional, narrative reviews. Our approach is best described as a narrative review 'informed' by social science versions of the systematic review – in particular, 'adapted' and 'integrated' approaches (Victor, 2008). We began by defining the review's scope. We developed a protocol to guide our review; in this case, we developed a set of key questions to focus our reading. A search strategy was developed.

Data extraction was undertaken by members of the team, with synthesis being a collaborative process. A narrative form of synthesis was employed, involving the description of the findings of studies we examined. Many of the studies were qualitative. For this reason, we applied a thematic approach, identifying key themes/issues arising within the literature.

The following questions structured/guided our review:
1. How has the right to play for children and young persons with disabilities been researched?
2. What barriers to the play of children and young persons with disabilities are identified within the literature?
3. Has the 'voice' of children and young persons with disabilities been presented in existing research? When present, what methods were used?

Our approach to the literature search was necessarily dynamic and iterative. We ran numerous searches using the academic search engines: Scopus, ProQuest Central, Web of Science, PubMed, CINAHL, ERIC and Google Scholar. Where search engines permitted, we employed Boolean searches; where they did not, we applied similar principles when running searches. Key search terms included 'disability', 'child(ren)', 'disorder' 'disabled child', 'children with disabilities', 'play', 'playing', 'leisure', 'recreation' and various terms relevant to specific diagnostic categories in childhood (e.g. autism) and relevant to each of our four contexts, for example, 'school', 'playground/s', 'outdoor/s', 'built environment/s', 'home', 'family', 'friends', 'siblings', 'nature', 'nature play', 'natural environments', 'wild', 'adventure' and so on. We used Google to find non-governmental organisations promoting play and in particular play for children with disabilities. This approach also resulted in the discovery of a number of relevant reports, which provided us with additional citations.

We included in our review academic literature. This included books published by reputable academic publishers, chapters in edited collections, journal articles and final reports from funded research. Conference proceedings were included only if they were formally published. Our key criteria for assessing 'quality' for this type of literature was whether it had been subject to peer review at some point. Grey literature was also included: reports produced by non-governmental organisations (e.g. Play England, Save the Children), reports written by professional bodies and reports produced by government agencies. Our key criterion for assessing 'quality' for this type of literature was whether it was evidence based.

7 Findings

Our review identified a series of barriers to play for children with disabilities. Barriers to play are an outcome of the relationship between the environment and the person, so the review acknowledges the everyday impact of children's impairment as an influencing factor. For example, many children with disabilities may experience some limitations in their activities due to a narrow margin of health or because enabling technologies do not exist as yet. These influences operate in conjunction with the environmental barriers that they encounter. Therefore, they are reported here under the heading of activity performance and play preferences in acknowledgement that all play activity is a combination of the interaction between the individual and the environment. The key barriers identified relate to:
- Activity performance and play preferences
- Physical barriers
- Social barriers – attitudes and behaviours

In what follows, we elaborate these barriers, which were found to operate in all four contexts.

7.1 Activity performance and play preferences

Impairments, activity limitations and participation restrictions can contribute to difficulties that children encounter within play. For example, studies of/with children for whom co-ordination is a challenge, for instance those who have been labelled as having Developmental Co-ordination Disorder (DCD), report that these children experience social exclusion in outdoor play activities because they find it difficult to join their peers in similar physical play activities (Poulsen, Ziviani and Cuskelly 2007). Children with physical impairments may have movement challenges, which represent barriers to their participation in play (Law et al., 2004), while the lack of provision of suitable equipment that enables a child to grasp objects can reduce their opportunities for play (Hsieh-Chun, 2012; Kernan, 2007; Mihaylov et al., 2004; Moyles, 2013). Children with autism spectrum disorders (ASDs) have been shown to experience significant difficulties in sensory processing that impact on their ability to participate in daily activities including social play (Baker et al., 2008; Baranek et al., 2006; Ben-Sasson et al., 2009; Tomcheck and Dunn, 2007; Wetherby and Woods, 2006). Children who have socio-emotional disabilities may have difficulty initiating and/or maintaining social interaction considered 'appropriate' to other children (Hestenes and Carroll, 2000). Although each childhood condition has not been studied extensively, there is a significant evidence here that characteristics of specific disabilities can and do shape activity, and specific attention to analysis of these barriers is needed.

Although there is little research that includes the views/perspectives of children with disabilities, the small amount of literature of this type raises important issues and questions regarding the impact of impairment on play preferences and experiences. For example, a Finnish study shows that children who have autism express their play preferences through their play choices. They often select sensorimotor and imitation play (Kangas Määttä and Uusiautti, 2012). Another study from Brazil indicates that children who have ADHD prefer play that does not involve rules or play partners (Pfeifer et al., 2011). These studies suggest that play preferences may be linked to the abilities of the child and that children with different impairments may have different aspirations for play. Understanding children's play preferences, the extent to which these are shaped by their impairment and/or other factors, is an issue worthy of further investigation. Currently, there is insufficient knowledge/evidence regarding the play needs and aspirations of children with different impairments. The existing research prompts additional questions such as whether, for example, the preference of children who have autism for solitary play should be enabled, or whether they should be encouraged towards more social play. Does respecting children's 'right to play' mean respecting their right to play entirely freely at all times? Families, health workers and educators may continue to promote the play-as-progress agenda; however, for children with disabilities, this also needs to include the child's right to experience play on his/her own terms. Squaring this circle is challenging.

In other studies, researchers found that children with different disabilities sought challenge and play partners in a community playground and enjoyed social play (Burke, 2012). In a study of access and usability of playgrounds in Sweden, however, researchers found that children with a range of disabilities reported that they wished for more interaction with other children (Prellwitz and Skar, 2007). These different findings in relation to play preferences show many play patterns similar to the play of 'typical' children. Children with disabilities, who frequently rely on adults to orchestrate play for them, however, may play in settings or with people that/who might not be their preferred choice. Issues of social inclusion or segregation, mixed ability or similar ability play come into consideration. Further research is needed to build a body of evidence on play preferences of children with disabilities from these perspectives.

7.2 Physical barriers – accessibility and usability

The concept of universal design goes far beyond physical accessibility to include much broader issues of social inclusion socio-economics, enabling human agency and *usability* (see UNCRPD, Article 2). Physical accessibility to sites/locations for play remains, however, a logical precursor to play itself. If the physical environment is not accessible for children with disabilities, they will be excluded from the environment. This exclusion is thought to reinforce negative attitudinal barriers towards children with disabilities (Atmakur, 2013). Although all European countries have adopted and ratified the UNCRC, the right to play has not been universally supported in state legislation or policy to remove barriers in the built environment. Consequently, different nation states are at different stages in enacting play policy and directing national resources for play provision. For example, in a 2003 project on public play provision for children with disabilities (Webb, 2003), it was noted that only two international pieces of legislation existed at the time related to playgrounds: the UK's DDA (Disability Discrimination Act, 1995) and the USA's ADA (Americans with Disabilities Act, 1990). While this situation is improving, there appears to be a definite gap between international rights of the child and the operationalising of their rights into legislation and policy for universal play and social inclusion in public play spaces. Legislative and policy gaps result in barriers to rights-based play provision in Europe. Further research is needed to establish how different countries in Europe are developing policy to promote play in relation to universal design and the physical environment.

A key barrier in establishing children's rights to play relates to the lack of knowledge and experience of disability and universal design among service providers and landscape architects or designers (Dunn and Moore, 2005; Prellwitz and Tamm, 1999; Woolley, 2013). In one study, planners or providers of playgrounds were found to have inadequate knowledge/understanding of universal design. This was compounded by poor communication in the planning process, a lack of clear guidelines and, most importantly, lack of consultation with persons with disabilities (Prellwitz and Tamm, 1999).

Another important finding from research is that 'getting it right' in the design of play spaces to enable children with disabilities to play can be challenging. Where 'special' accessible features are included in design, playground amenity officers in the United Kingdom, for example, have reported that this can also lead to segregation (Dunn and Moore, 2005). Planning needs to be for inclusion – for environments that are usable, not just physically accessible: 'activity rather than appliance oriented design creates a setting where all children may be included in the fun' (Christensen, 2002).

Physical barriers also refer to the characteristics of a physical setting that promotes or limits play. Observations by Rigby and Gaik (2007), in three different environments of children with physical impairments, show that where environmental conditions are less supportive, children with physical impairments are least playful. They highlighted the influence of the physical environment in determining and shaping play opportunities. Their research also emphasised the importance of availability, accessibility and usability of play materials. The specific characteristics of the physical environment that produce barriers to participation are numerous, but include noise, crowding, temperature, lighting, design and accessibility, depending on the child's specific needs (Law et al., 1999; Rimmer et al., 2004).

Some studies suggest that the home setting is best for supporting playfulness, when compared to school or community settings, with environmental barriers increasing with age as the child expands his or her horizon into more varied community and recreational settings (Law et al., 2007; Rigby and Gaik, 2007). Other studies, however, point to physical barriers within the home, highlighting how children often require assistance transferring between play spaces in the home (e.g. up/down stairs). In some homes, there is not enough room for wheelchairs to manoeuvre about or enough room to accommodate visits from friends due to the space taken up by assistive technologies and other equipment (Brotherson et al., 2008; Connors and Stalker, 2003; Geisthardt et al., 2002). Almost three decades ago, Lewis (1987) highlighted the reality that some parents may delay in adapting the home environment due to difficulty in coming to terms with their child's disability. Anecdotal evidence from professional health practitioners suggests that this is still an ongoing issue. Thus, the home space can also be a physical barrier to play, in terms of inaccessibility, especially in early years of childhood before any adaptations are made to the home's physical layout.

Literature notes that physical barriers to children's play also occur in schools, where older school buildings in some countries are not designed for wheelchair accessibility (Santer et al., 2007), and outdoor school playgrounds are all too often constructed for 'typically' developing children and are not easily accessible for children with physical impairments (Rigby and Gaik, 2007). Indeed, with regard to outdoor play, children with disabilities have been found to be 'under represented users of public open spaces and play spaces' (Woolley, 2013, pp. 451).

All sorts of benefits to children (with and without disabilities) of playing outdoors, including play in and with 'nature', have been identified (Blakesley et al., 2013; Kuo and Faber Taylor, 2004; Pavey, 2006). Children acquire life skills through playing outside in their communities, such as sharing, looking out for one another and asking for help (Beunderman, 2010). Most importantly, playing outdoors has a significant place in most children's lives and is typically a setting for social inclusion.

To date, the focus for considering outdoor play spaces for children with disabilities has, primarily, been on the physical accessibility of public, built playground environments (e.g. Moore and Lynch, 2015; Webb, 2003). Three Swedish studies, for example, found that children with disabilities were deprived of play on/in playgrounds due to physical inaccessibility and limited usability (Prellwitz and Skar, 2007, Prellwitz et al., 2001; Prellwitz and Tamm, 1999). In Prellwitz and Skar's study (2007), sand significantly limited mobility; play equipment was too small for wheelchair users and some children with cognitive impairments/disabilities to use. For children with visual impairments/disabilities, grey wood play equipment and lack of visual markings limited their access to play, and some play equipments were too complicated to understand. This resulted in children developing other strategies, frequently through fear. Afraid to be seen to use the equipment in the 'wrong way', they waited until nobody else was on the playground before having a 'go' (Prellwitz and Skar, 2007).

Although access to nature is included in the UNCRC, it has been acknowledged that it is all too often a forgotten human right and one that needs to be addressed for all children (Anderson-Brolin, 2002), but acutely for children with disabilities.

Studies of children with ADD/HD, for example, found that there is a direct relationship with green spaces and attention: spending time in nature promotes better attention and decreases symptoms of ADHD (Kuo and Taylor, 2004; Taylor, Kuo and Sullivan, 2001). While, again, this type of finding is at risk of prioritising the 'play-as-progress' concept, denial of a right to nature play is arguably a denial of the right to the benefits of this type of play and thus of concern.

Policy documents and guidelines for built environments for children with disabilities typically do not include natural elements (e.g. Canadian Coalition for accessible play-spaces, 2014; DESSA, 2007). Hence, designing for inclusion has tended not to incorporate ways to access nature as a core feature, and this has resulted in further barriers in the physical environment for children with disabilities.

7.3 Social barriers – attitudes and behaviours

Even when the physical environment has been built or adapted to maximise accessibility, it may still operate as a social exclusion area (Dunn et al., 2003). Often this is because of social and/or attitudinal barriers. Literature suggests that while professionals, parents and peers can all play important roles in facilitating and empowering play for children with disabilities, their attitudes and/or behaviours can also, at times, impact negatively on the play experiences of these children.

Research suggests that children with disabilities can experience social exclusion from their peers; they are not always invited to play with friends or are not always encouraged/supported to invite friends to come over to their houses to play (Mundhenke et al., 2010; Sandberg et al., 2004). Parents of children with disabilities have reported problems with bullying and difficulties that other (non-disabled) children have in knowing how to play with their children (Oates et al., 2011; Preece and Jordan, 2009). In addition, studies have shown that children with ASD, for example, who have fewer playdates organised for them in the home have more difficulties in negotiating play with peers in the school playground (Frankel et al., 2011). There is evidence to suggest, however, that even when inclusive, collaborative play is facilitated, and it is not always a positive experience for the children with disabilities. The non-disabled children tend to take the lead in the play, while the children with disabilities become onlookers, particularly in outdoor play, where the activities might be more physically demanding (Rigby and Gaik, 2007).

How to address children with disabilities' exclusion by peers is an under-researched topic. Where it has been considered, the challenge it poses for practitioners is made clear. Spencer-Cavaliere and Watkinson (2010) found that the children with disabilities in their study reported not being asked to play by other children and being told that they were not welcome to take part and that this led to them not being included. Children stated that gaining entry to less-structured play environments – such as play within recess – was particularly challenging. Taub and

Greer (2000) found that children with physical impairments/disabilities not only valued their unstructured play experiences but also reported being excluded by their peers. This highlights what appears to be a major difficulty in the promotion of play for children with disabilities: how to promote children with disabilities' engagement with inclusive, 'free play', while not intervening in that play to such a degree that it is no longer 'free'. For example, in a school setting, Hestenes and Caroll (2000) found that the presence of a teacher was a significant predictor of children's inclusive interactions.

Teachers can initiate play between children with and without disabilities (Odom et al., 1996) and facilitate continued play in part by modelling appropriate behaviour for individual children (Odom et al. 1993) and in part by supervising play. It is clear that a teacher's presence and support can impact positively on the frequency with which inclusive interactions occur. Yet this type of play is usually 'structured'. How adults might facilitate inclusion in free play opportunities – if to be 'free', the play must be child directed and determined – is less well understood. Identifying relevant strategies to support inclusive 'free play' is a major challenge for practitioners and warrants further investigation by researchers.

Within school settings, there is some evidence that teachers, particularly those who specialise in 'special educational needs', do not always encourage and support children with disabilities to engage in a various forms of play: investigative and manipulative, imaginative, construction, play with natural materials and outside play (Ozen et al., 2013). Within such settings, children with disabilities may not be given the same opportunities as their peers to make choices, to take risks, to accept challenges or to make friends (Richardson, 2002). Further, Buchanon and Johnson (2009) and Richardson (2002) considered that without knowledgeable and sensitive professionals, a 'fix and serve' educational policy is delivered that often denies the opportunity for play.

Other attitudes held by a range of professionals can be barriers to the play of children with disabilities (Cross et al., 2004). For example, Ludvigsen et al. (2005) found staff at an outdoor adventure play recreation site attempting to stop disabled children engaging in 'messy' activities such as kicking and throwing leaves, perhaps reflecting the heightened control of disabled children (Curran and Runswick-Cole, 2013). Furthermore, Ludvigsen et al. (2005) also found that parents (of children with disabilities) although initially positive about the idea of adventure play, perceived the play site to be 'unsafe'. So perceptions of 'risk' also figure highly. Gleave (2010) supports this point, reporting that staff at outdoor recreation sites considered less supervised outdoor opportunities to be 'too risky' for disabled children.

Sometimes, the presence of a parent in a play situation is less about parental attitudes and more about necessity. For example, in a study by Prellwitz and Skar (2007), children were found to need parental assistance to move around and use playground equipment since the design of the playground did not support their independent mobility. The children indicated, however, that they would have liked to have been able to use the playground without an adult being present. Parents themselves are sometimes aware that being with their children in playgrounds contributed to their children feeling stigmatised. Their 'solution' to this problem, however, was sometimes to avoid playgrounds, thus leading to further exclusion of their children from play opportunities (Prellwitz, 2007).

Children with disabilities rely on the home social environment for much of their play opportunities; they tend to have fewer friends and spend more time with adults than other children (Skar, 2002 and Tamm, 2005 cited in Mundhenke et al., 2010). Parent's perceptions of risk in this setting can, however, also be a barrier to play for their children. Connors and Stalker (2003) found that parents could be a barrier to friends coming over to play and sometimes applied restrictions for the purpose of 'protection' and avoidance of risk. Parental perceptions of risk have also been found to restrict children with disabilities' play within natural environments. Parents have been found to attribute additional 'vulnerability' to their children with disabilities, with unintended negative consequences (Gleave, 2010). Children with disabilities have themselves reported experiencing 'over-protection', which precluded their opportunities for creativity, risk and physical challenge, all essentials for play (Andrews, 2012).

8 Discussion and Conclusion

The last three decades have seen unprecedented levels of international acknowledgement, from a human rights perspective, of the rights of children and young persons (UNCRC, 1989) and all persons with disabilities (UNCRPD, 2008). For the first time in world history, all children under the UNCRC have a right to play, enshrined in international law. This was reinforced by General Comment 17 (2013) where children and young persons with disabilities were identified as a group 'vulnerable' in relation to the realisation of their play rights. Despite this acknowledgement, however, there remains much to be done at national levels, not least for EU member states in relation to the development, implementation and evaluation of national play policies.

With regard to the play and recreational barriers affecting children and young persons with disabilities, the characteristics of specific impairments/disabilities significantly contribute to the limitations and the barriers experience in their play (Tonkin, 2014) and can contribute to certain play preferences. For example, children with physical impairments/disabilities may have movement challenges (Law et al., 2004), children with autism spectrum disorders may experience difficulties participating in social play (Ben-Sasson et al. 2009) and children with socio-emotional disabilities may have difficulty initiating and/or maintaining social interaction with their peers (Hestenes and Carroll, 2000). These 'impairment effects' as they might be termed should not be ignored. Because the range of 'disabilities' albeit grouped within certain categorical terms, for example, physical, communicative and cognitive disabilities is broad, so too is the range of 'barriers' children and young people with disabilities encounter when engaging in play and recreation. Many of these barriers are unique to individual children. We suggest that further research, policy development and Universal Design implementation must keep this reality at the forefront of their work. Researching with children is central to this work to ensure their 'voice' is heard and that they are participating in matters that are important to them. Our review of existing research suggests that the 'voice' of children with disabilities is all too often absent within research. Of course, quite what is meant by 'voice' in this regard is a complex question, as is how to enable and 'capture' their 'voice' in meaningful ways. As yet there are no universally agreed answers to either question or 'universal solutions' or 'ideal methodology', which addresses these issues completely (Lewis and Porter, 2007). We need to continuously develop innovative approaches.

It is further evidenced within the literature reviewed that there is an imbalance in the examination of play and recreation for children and young persons who have different impairments/disabilities. There are more studies focusing on physical disabilities (Clark and MacArthur, 2008; Cook and Melvyn, 1999; Cooper et al., 2004; Kalyvas and Reid, 2003; Newacheck et al., 2004; Newacheck and Halfon, 1998; Rubin et al., 2014; Schreuer et al., 2014; Shikako-Thomas et al., 2013) and autism spectrum disorder (Anderson et al., 2004; Barton and Wolery, 2008; Cook and Melvyn, 1999; Machalicek et al., 2008) than any other impairment/disability 'category'.

Evidence-based studies or key findings on other impairments such as cognitive disabilities, communication disabilities, hearing disabilities, visual disabilities or multiple disabilities are scarce (Cook and Melvyn, 1999). We suggest, therefore, that this imbalance needs to be addressed at national policy levels and by research funders. Further research is required that identifies and understands the barriers to play for children and young persons with cognitive and communication difficulties in particular.

Many of us live in a risk-averse society (Barron, 2014) with 'risk reduction' being viewed as a positive goal. This 'risk reduction' rhetoric appears to be interwoven within much of the research and literature reviewed relating to play and recreation for children and young persons with disabilities. The issue is not dissimilar vis-à-vis children without disabilities, but more acute for children with disabilities. Livingstone (2002) argues that children and young people need opportunities to interact with the world in their play and recreation and to assist in the development of personal autonomy and independence. We support the need to balance risk in children and young people's play worlds and endorse the views expressed in General Comment 17 in this regard:

> While children must not be exposed to harm in the realization of their rights under article 31, some degree of risk and challenge is integral to play and recreational activities and is a necessary component of the benefits of these activities. (General Comment 17, pp. 12)

Because the reality of 'risk-averse' societies is a relatively new phenomenon and is not universal, the ramifications for children's development, independence and loss of benefits from activities are not yet known (Barron, 2014). Rather than viewing society as 'risk averse', we suggest viewing the play and recreation for children and young people from a 'benefits' perspective, that is, the benefits of play and recreation for children and young persons with disabilities far exceed the potential risks in most instances.

We also note that there is, of course, a much broader range of 'barriers' that impact on the play experiences of children with disabilities. Socio-economic factors are known to impact on the lives of children with disabilities more broadly and in relation to their play experiences (Bedell, 2011). This is, however, another under-researched issue warranting further investigation. The lack of accessible and affordable transport is also known to be a barrier to children with disabilities and their families engaging in leisure activities (Bedell et al., 2013). Finally, little research has examined how social class or socio-economic factors, gender, ethnicity and geographical location intersect with diverse impairments/disabilities, resulting in quite different experiences for children. Research is needed that recognises and explores the heterogeneity of children with disabilities experiences and the different barriers that they may face.

8.1 Barriers in Home, Educational, Built and Natural Settings

The following is the summary of main barriers to play and recreation for children and young persons with disabilities and gaps in existing research in this area:
- Too few studies of children's own play preferences or play forms
- Existing studies focus on the needs of children with a physical impairment/disability. Need to understand barriers to play of children with a range of impairments/disabilities
- In some countries, there is a lack of clear legislation and policy in relation to built environments and accessible and usable spaces for play
- In some countries, there is a lack of clear legislation and policy in relation to including nature and important natural features in built play environments and playgrounds and support for nature play for all
- Insufficient consultation with stakeholders (children and young people with disabilities and their families and friends), and lack of disability equality training in key professionals who lead on planning, design and policy can hamper the development of inclusive play
- Lack of information on specific strategies to address barriers to participation in home, school and community activities again can hamper inclusive play

9 Recommendations

1. We support the recent views expressed in General Comment 17 for the need for mechanisms to monitor and evaluate national initiatives, which strive to achieve national obligations under Article 31, such as a National Play Policy. This will provide each nation with a more in-depth understanding of the extent and nature of children and young persons with disabilities' engagement in play and recreation.

2. As evidenced by our review, there is literature identifying barriers to children and young persons with disabilities who engage in play and recreation. On closer examination, however, too much of this involves little or no consultation with children and young people, their carers or parents.

The 'voice' of children and young persons with disabilities is almost absent from play studies, and this needs serious attention in any research or policy related to play and recreation. Children have the right to have their voice heard in any matter which concerns them, and this deficit has already been acknowledged by the UNCRC. This includes the requirement to identify and develop effective methodologies ensuring the child is enabled to communicate in the way that maximises his/her potential to participate. Similarly, the disabled people's movement has long campaigned for the concept of emancipatory and participatory research on the basis of 'nothing about us without us', and this applies as much to research with children with disabilities as it does to adults.

3. Best practice guidelines for design and provision of inclusive settings need to be established to reduce the environmental barriers that limit the access to and enjoyment of play and recreation by children with disabilities. Such guidelines need to be informed by an understanding of the environment that includes but advances beyond the purely physical.

Policy needs to be informed by the users, that is children with disabilities and their families, if it is to be evidence based. A holistic approach to design is essential to incorporate natural and built elements and to consider both accessible and usable components in planning and provision.

Guidelines for local authorities and other bodies responsible for developing play opportunities for all children need to include reference to the needs of children with disabilities and provide tools for 'auditing' existing play provision for children with disabilities. Inspiring examples of best practice are needed to support the development of such guidelines and assessment tools.

4. Risk avoidance is a recurrent theme within much of the literature about play and recreation for children and young persons with disabilities, in all settings considered (home, educational settings, the built and natural environment). While concerns about danger and injury are understandable, some degree of risk and challenge is

fundamental to play and recreational activities and is a necessary component of the benefits of these activities. Research on play contexts for children with disabilities needs to apply a risk versus benefits approach.

5. The characteristics of specific impairments/disabilities do contribute to the limitations and barriers children and young persons with disabilities experience in their play (Tonkin, 2014). There is no one solution to overcoming these barriers, rather we recommend a transdisciplinary approach involving the children and young persons themselves, parents, professionals, relevant organisational bodies and policy makers in addressing the unique as well as the generic barriers to play opportunities for all children and young persons with disabilities.

6. Due to an imbalance within literature on the topic of play and recreation for children and young persons with disabilities, we suggest that a stronger focus needs to be placed on the experiences and needs of children and young persons with cognitive impairments or disabilities, communication difficulties, hearing impairments, visual impairments and/or multiple impairments (Cook and Melvyn, 1999).

References

Allen, S. 2008. Finding Home: Challenges Faced by Geographically Mobile Families. *Family Relations*, 57 (1), pp. 84–99.

Aitken, S.C. 2001. *Geographies of young people: the morally contested spaces of identity*. London: Routledge.

Americans with Disabilities Act of 1990,Pub. L. No. 101-336, § 2, 104 Stat 328. 1991

Anaby, D., Law, M., Hanna, S. and DeMatteo, C. 2012. Predictors of change in participation rates following acquired brain injury: Results of a longitudinal study. *Developmental Medicine and Child Neurology*, 54, pp. 339-346.

Anderson-Brolin, L. 2002. *Children's right to a good physical environment: Central concepts and problem definition*. Stockholm: Save the Children Sweden

Anderson, A., Moore, D.W., Godfrey, R. and Fletcher-Flinn, C.M. 2004. Social skills assessment of children with autism in free-play situations, *Autism*, 8 (4), pp. 369-385.

Andrews, M. 2012. *Exploring play for early childhood studies*. London: Sage.

Atmakur, S. 2013. Focus: playgrounds of exclusion. State of the World's Children 2013. Children with Disabilities. Available at: http://www.unicef.org/sowc2013/focus_playgrounds_of_inclusion.html [Accessed 25th July 2015].

Baker, A. E., Lane, A., Angley, M. T. and Young, R. L. 2008. The relationship between sensory processing patterns and behavioral responsiveness in autistic disorder: A pilot study. *Journal of Autism and Developmental Disorders*, 38 (5), pp. 867-875.

Baranek, G., David, F., Poe, M., Stone, W. and Watson, L., 2006. Sensory experience questionnaire: Discriminating sensory features in young children with autism, developmental delays and typical development. *Journal of Child Psychology and Psychiatry, 47 (6)*, pp. 591-601.

Barron, C. 2013. Súgradh Newsletter. A Celebration of National Play Day 1, pp. 1-10.

Barron, C. 2013. Physical activity play in local housing estates and child wellness in Ireland. *International Journal of Play, 2* (3), pp. 220-236,

Barron, C. 2014. 'I had no credit to ring you back': Children's strategies of negotiation and resistance to parental surveillance via mobile phones. *Surveillance and Society, 12* (3) pp. 401-413.

Barton, E. E. and Wolery, M. 2008. Teaching pretend play to children with disabilities. A review to the literature. *Topics in Early Childhood, 28* (2), pp. 109-125.

Benjamin, D. 1995. 'Afterword'. *IN* Benjamin, D.N., Stea, D. and Saille, D. (eds) *The Home: Words, Interpretations, Meanings and Environments*. Aldershot: Avebury.

Ben-Sasson, A., Hen, L,. Fluss, R., Cermak, S. Engel-Yeger, B. and Gal, E. 2009. A meta-analysis of sensory modulation symptoms in individuals with autism spectrum disorders. *Journal of Autism and Developmental Disorders, 39*, pp. 1-11.

Beunderman, J. 2010. *People Make Play: the impact of staffed play provision on children, families and communities*. London: Play England.

Blakesley, D., Rickinson, M. and Dillon, J. 2013. *Engaging children on the autistic spectrum with the natural environment: Teacher insight study and evidence review*. Natural England Commissioned Report NECR 116. London, Natural England.

Bluebond-Langer, M. and Korbin, J.E. 2007. Challenges and opportunities in the anthropology of childhoods: An introduction to "Children, Childhoods, and Childhood Studies". *American Anthropologist, 109* (2), pp. 241-246.

Brotherson, M. J., Cook, C. C., Erwin, E. J. and Weigel, C. J. 2008. Understanding self-determination and families of young children with disabilities in home environments. *Journal of Early Intervention, 31,* pp. 22–43.

Buchanon, M. and Johnson, T.G. 2009. A Second look at play for Young Children with Disabilities. *American Journal of Play, 2* (1), pp. 41-59.

Burke, C. 2005. "Play in focus". Children researching their own spaces and places for play. *Children, Youth and Environment, 15* (1), pp. 27-53.

Burke, J. 2012. 'Some kids climb up; some kids climb down': culturally constructed play-worlds of children with impairments, *Disability and Society, 27* (7), pp. 965-981.

Canadian Coalition for Accessible Playspaces. 2014. *Accessible Playspaces in Canada: A guidebook for children's playspaces that are accessible to persons with disabilities based on CAN/CSA-Z614: Annex H.* Available from:

http://www.allabilitieswelcome.ca/Playspaces/files/Annex_H_Guidebook.pdf [Accessed 12th August 2015].

Carver, S., Evans, A. and Fritz, S. 2002. Wilderness Attribute Mapping in the United Kingdom, *International Journal of Wilderness, 8* (1), pp. 24–29.

Christensen, K. 2002. *Creating inclusive outdoor play environments; designing for ability rather than disability.*

http://www.adventureislandplayground.org/Keith%20Christensen%20article.PDF. [Accessed 10 Sep 2015]

Clark, P. and MacArthur, J. 2008. Children with physical disability: Gaps in service provision problems joining in. *Journal of Paediatrics and Child Health*, 44 (7-8), pp. 455-58.

Cook, B. G. and Semmel, M.I. 1999. Peer Acceptance of Included Students with Disabilities as a Function of Severity of Disability and Classroom Composition. *Journal of Special Education,* 33 (1), pp. 50-61.

Cooper, D. M., Nemet, D. and Galassetti, P. 2004. Exercise, stress, and inflammation in the growing child: from the bench to the playground. *Current Opinion in Pediatrics*, 16 (3), pp. 286-292.

Connors, C. and Stalker, K. 2003. *The Views and Experiences of Disabled Children and Their Siblings: A Positive Outlook.* London: Jessica Kingsley Publishers.

Cross, A., Traub, E. K., Hutter-Pishgahi, L. and Shelton, G. 2004. Elements of Successful Inclusion for Children with Significant Disabilities. *Topics in Early Childhood Special Education, 24* (3), pp. 169-183.

Curran, T. and Runswick-Cole, K. (eds) 2013. *Disabled Children's Childhood Studies.* Basingstoke: Palgrave Macmillan.

DESSA. 2007. *Play for all: providing play facilities for disabled children.* Dublin: DESSA.

Dockett, S. and Perry, B. 2005. 'You need to know how to play safe': children's experiences of starting school. *Contemporary Issues in Early Childhood*, 6 (1), pp. 4-18.

Dunn, K. and Moore, M. 2005. Developing accessible play space in the UK: a social model approach. *Children, Youth and Environments*, 15 (1), pp. 331-354.

Edmonds, E. and Pavcnik, N. 2005. Child labor in the global economy. *Journal of Economic Perspectives*, 19 (1), pp. 199-220.

Einarsdottir, J. 2005. We can decide what to play! : children's perception of quality in an Icelandic playschool. *Early Education and Development*, 16 (4), pp. 469-488.

Engel-Yeger, B., Jams, T., Anaby, D. and Law, M. 2009. Differences in patterns of participation between youths with cerebral palsy and typically developing peers. *American Journal of Occupational Therapy*, 63, pp. 96-104.

Fjørtoft, I. 2004, Landscape and Play: The effects of natural environments on children's play and motor development. *Children, Youth and Environments*, 14 (2), pp. 21–44.

Frankel, F., Gorospe, C., Chang, Y. and Sugar, C. 2011. Mothers' reports of play dates and observation of school playground behavior of children having high-functioning autism spectrum disorders. *Journal of Child Psychology and Psychiatry, 52* (5), pp. 571-579.

Garvey, C. 1990. *Play.* USA: Harvard University Press.

Geisthardt, C. L., Brotherson, M. and Cook, C. 2002. Friendships of Children with Disabilities in the Home Environment. *Education and Training in Mental Retardation and Developmental Disabilities, 37* (3), pp. 235-52.

Goodley, D. and Runswick-Cole, C. 2010. Emancipating Play: Dis/abled Children, Development and Deconstruction. *Disability and Society*, 25 (4), pp. 499-512.

Handy, S.L., Boarnet, M., Ewing, R. and Killingsworth, R.E. 2002. How the built environment affects physical activity: views from urban planning. *American Journal of Preventive Medicine*, 23(2), Suppl 1, pp. . 64–73.

Harpur, P. 2012. Embracing the new disability rights paradigm: the importance of the Convention on the Rights of Persons with Disabilities. *Disability and Society*, 27 (1), pp. 1–14.

Hartley, S. and Newton, C. 2009. Children with developmental disabilities in the majority of the world. *IN:* Shevell, M. (ed.) *Neurodevelopmental disabilities: clinical and scientific foundations*. London: Mac Keith Press

Heah, T., Case, T., McGuire, B, and M. Law. 2007. Successful participation: the lived experience among children with disabilities. Canadian Journal of Occupational Therapy. 74(1), pp.38-47

Henricks, T. 2008. The nature of play: an Overview. *American Journal of Play, 1* (2), pp. 157-180.

Henricks, T. 2015. *Play and the Human Condition*. Chicago: University of Illinois Press.

Hestenes, L. and Carroll, C. 2000. The play interactions of young children with and without disabilities: Individual and environmental influences. *Early Childhood Research Quarterly*, 15 (2), pp. 229–246.

Hilton, C. L., Crouch, M. C. and Israel, H. 2008. Out-of-school participation patterns in children with high-functioning autism spectrum disorders. *American Journal of Occupational Therapy*, 62, pp. 554-563.

Hsieh-Chun, H. 2012. Effectiveness of adaptive pretend play on affective expression and imagination of children with cerebral palsy. *Research in Developmental Difficulties*, 29, pp. 459-466.

Imms, C. 2008. Children with Cerebral Palsy Participate: A Review of the Literature. *Disability and Rehabilitation, 30* (24), pp. 1867–1884.

Imms, C., Reilly, S., Carlin, J. and Dodd, K. 2008. Diversity of participation in children with cerebral palsy. *Developmental Medicine and Child Neurology*, 50, pp. 363-369.

International Play Association (IPA). 2015. The Play Rights of Children with Disabilities. Position Paper. Available at: http://ipaworld.org/wp-content/uploads/2015/08/IPA-Disabled-Children-Position-Stmt.pdf [Accessed 4th September 2015].

Iwarsson, S. and Stahl, A. 2003. Accessibility, usability and universal design- positioning and definition of concepts describing person-environment relationships. *Disability and Rehabilitation*, 25 (2), pp. 57-66.

Kangas, S., Määttä, K. and Uusiautti, S. 2012. Alone and in a group: ethnographic research on autistic children's play. *International Journal of Play*, 1 (1), pp. 37-50.

Kaplan, I. 2008. Being "seen" being "heard"; engaging with students on the margins of education through participatory photography *IN*: Thompson, P. (ed.) *Doing visual research with children and young people*. London: Routledge Taylor and Francis Group.

Kernan, M. 2007. Play as a context for Learning Play Ireland. Available at: http://www.ncca.ie/en/Curriculum_and_Assessment/Early_Childhood_and_Primary_Education/Early_Childhood_Education/How_Aistear_was_developed/Research_Papers/Play_paper.pdf [Accessed 10th September 2015].

King, G., Law, M., Hurley, P., Petrenchik, T. and Schwellnus, H. 2010. A developmental comparison of the out-of-school recreation and leisure activity participation of boys and girls with and without physical disabilities. International *Journal of Disability, Development and Education*, 57, pp. 77-107.

King, G., McDougall, J., DeWit, D., Petrenchik, T., Hurley, P. and Law, M. 2009. Predictors of change over time in the activity participation of children and youth with physical disabilities. *Children's Health Care*, 38 (4), pp. 321-351.

Kline, S. 2004. Learners, spectators, or gamers? An investigation of the impact of digital media in the media-saturated household *IN*: Goldstein, J., Buckingham, D. and Brougere, G. (eds.) *Toys, Games and Media*. New York: Lawrence Erlbaum Associates.

Kraemer, B. R., Blacher, J. and Marshal, M. P. 1997. Adolescents with severe disabilities: Family, school, and community integration. *Journal of the Association for Persons with Severe Handicaps*, 22, pp. 224-234.

Kuo, F. and Faber, T. 2004. A potential natural treatment for Attention-Deficit Hyperactivity disorder: evidence from a national study. *American Journal of Public Health*, 94, pp. 1580-1586.

La Fontaine, J. 1997. Are Children People? Paper presented at International Conference on Anthropology and Children. May 1997. Linkoping University, Sweden. Available from: http://liu.diva-portal.org/smash/get/diva2:510945/FULLTEXT01.pdf [Accessed August 28th 2015].

Law, M., Anaby, D., Teplicky, R., Khetani, M. and Coster, W. 2013. Participation in the home environment among children and youth with and without disabilities. British Journal of Occupational Therapy, 76 (2), 58-66.

Law, M., Petrenchik, T., King, G., and Hurley, P. 2007. Perceived environmental barriers to recreational, community, and school participation for children and youth with physical disabilities. *Archives for Physical and Medical Rehabilitation*, 88, 1636- 1642

Law, M., Finkelman, S., Hurley, P., Rosenbaum, P., King, S., King, G. and Hanna, S. 2004. Participation of children with physical disabilities: Relationships with diagnosis, physical function, and demographic variables. *Scandinavian Journal of Occupational Therapy*, 11, pp. 156-162.

Law, M., Haight, M., Milroy, B., Williams, D., Stewart, D. and Rosenbaum, P. 1999. Environmental factors affecting the occupations of children with physical disabilities. *Journal of Occupational Science*, 6, pp. 102-110.

Lester, S. and Maudsley, M. 2007. *Play naturally: a review of children's natural play*. London. National Children's Bureau. Play England.

Le Vine, R. 2007. Ethnographic studies of childhood: a historical overview. *American Anthropologist*, 109 (2), pp. 247-260.

Lewis, B. 1987. How are families managing at home? Architectural barriers in households of children with special needs- an issue ignored by health professional. *Children's Environments Quarterly*, 4 (3), pp. 36-41.

Lewis, A. and Porter, J. 2007. Research and pupil voice. *IN*: L. Florian (ed) *The Sage Handbook of Special Education*. London: Sage. pp. 222-232.

Livingstone, S. 2002. *Young people and new media: Childhood and the changing media environment*. London: Sage Publications.

Ludvigsen A, Creegan, C. and Mills, H. 2005. *Let's Play Together: Play and Inclusion - Evaluation of Better Play Round Three*. Barnardo's. Available at: www.barnardos.org.uk/lets_play_together_report.pdf [Accessed 31 Mar 2015].

Majnemer, A., Shevell, M., Law, M., Birnbaum, R., Chilingaryan, G., Rosenbaum, P. and Poulin, C. 2008. Participation and enjoyment of leisure activities in school-aged children with cerebral palsy. *Developmental Medicine and Child Neurology*, 50 (10), pp. 751-758.

Marshall, J.D. 2007. Urban Land Area and Population Growth: A New Scaling Relationship for Metropolitan Expansion. Urban Studies, 44 (10), pp. 1889-1904

Maulik, P.K. and Darmstadt, G. 2007. Childhood disability in low- and middle-income countries: overview of screening, prevention, services, legislation, and epidemiology. *Pediatrics*, 120 (Suppl 1), pp. S1-S55.

Mc Kendrick, J., Bradford, M. and Fielder, A. 2000. Making sense of the commercialisation of leisure space for children *IN* Valentine, G. and Holloway, S.L. (ds.) *Children's Geographies; playing, living, learning*. London: Routledge.

McManus, V., Corcoran, P. and Perry, I. J. 2008. Participation in everyday activities and quality of life in pre-teenage children living with cerebral palsy in South West Ireland. *BMC Pediatrics*, 8, Article 50.

Machalicek, W., O'Reilly, M.F., Beretvas, N., Sigafoos, J., Lancioni, G., Sorrells, A., Lang, R. and Rispoli, M. 2008. A review of school-based instructional interventions for students with autism spectrum disorders. *Research in Autism Spectrum Disorders*, 2 (3), pp. 395-416.

Meire, J. 2007. Qualitative research on children's play; a review of recent literature IN: Jambor, T. and Gils, J.V. (eds.) *Several Perspectives on Children's Play*. Antwerpen – Apeldoom: Garant.

Min, B. and Lee, J. 2006, Children's neighbourhood place as a psychological and behavioral domain. *Journal of environmental psychology, 26* (1), pp. 51-71.

Mihaylov, S.I., Jarvis, S.N., Colver, A.F. and Beresford, B. 2004. Identification and description of environmental factors that influence participation of children with cerebral palsy. *Developmental Medicine and Child Neurology 46* (5), pp. 299-304.

Mintz, S. 2009. Children's Culture. Paper Presented at the *Re-Staging Childhood Conference*. Utah, USA: Utah State University, August 2009.

Moore, A. and Lynch, H. 2015. Accessibility and usability of playground environments for children under 12: A scoping review'. *Scandinavian Journal of Occupational Therapy, 22* (5), pp. 331-334.

Moore, J. 2000. Placing home in context. *Journal of Environmental Psychology, 20 (3)*, 207-217.

Morrow, V. and Richards, M. 1996. The ethics of social research with children: an over view. *Children and Society*, 10 (2), 90-105.

Moyles, J. 2013, Play and Early Years, Play Wales. Available from: www.playwales.org [Accessed May 24th 2015].

Mundhenke, L., Hermansson, L. and Nattterland, B. 2010. Experiences of Swedish children with disabilities: activities and social support in daily life. *Scandinavian Journal of Occupational Therapy*, 17, 130-139.

National Children's Bureau. 2002. Fact Sheet No.4. Where Do Children Play? Available from: http://www.ncb.org.uk/media/124830/no.4_where_do_children_play.pdf [Accessed June 30th 2016].

Newacheck, P.W. and Halfon, N. 1998. Prevalence and impact of disabling chronic conditions in childhood. *American Journal of Public Heath*, 88 (4), pp. 610-617.

Newacheck, P.W., Inkelas, M. and Kim, S.E. 2004. Health services and health care expenditures for children with disabilities. *Pediatrics*, 114 (1),pp. 79-86.

Oates, A., Bebbington, A., Bourke, J. Girdler, S. and Leonard, H., 2011. Leisure participation for school-aged children with Down syndrome. *Disability and Rehabilitation*, 33(19-20), 1880-1889

Odom, S. L., McConnell, S.R. and Chandler, L.K. 1993. Acceptability and feasibility of classroom-based social interaction interventions for young children with disabilities. *Exceptional Children*, 60, pp. 226-236.

Odom, S. L., Peck, C. A., Hanson, M., Beckman, P. J., Kaiser, A. P., Lieber, J., Brown, W. H., Horn, E. M., and Schwartz, I. S. 1996. Inclusion at the preschool level: An ecological systems analysis. *Social Policy: Society for Research on Child Development, 10* (2 /3), pp. 18–30.

Ozen, A., Ergonekon, Y., Ulke-Kurkcuoglu, B. and Genç, D. 2013. Opinions of special education teachers about activity-based intervention. Hacettepe Üniversitesi *Journal of Education*, 44, pp. 262-274.

Nilsen, R. D. and Rogers, B. 2005. That's not a good idea mom: negotiating children's subjectivity while constructing 'home' as a research site. *Children's Geographies, 3,* pp. 345-362.

Pavey, B. 2006. *The forest school and inclusion: a project evaluation*. Available from: www.leeds.ac.uk/educol/documents/161165.doc . [Accessed 23rd August 2015].

Peirson, L., Fitzpatrick-Lewis, D., Morrison, K., Ciliska, D., Kenny, M., Usman Ali, M., and Raina, P. 2015. Prevention of overweight and obesity in children and youth: a systematic review and meta-analysis. Canadian Medical Association Journal Open. Available from: http://www.ncbi.nlm.nih.gov/pmc/articles/PMC4382039/, [Accessed 23rd August 2015]

Piaget, J. 1945. *Play, dreams and imitation in childhood*. London: Heinemann.

Pfeifer, L., Terra, L. N., Ferreira dos Santos, J. L.,Stagnitti, K. E. and Panuncio-Pinto, M. P. 2011. Play preference of children with ADHD and typically developing children in Brazil: A pilot study. *Australian Occupational Therapy Journal, 58*, pp. 419–428.

Poulsen, A. A., Ziviani, J. M. and Cuskelly, M. 2007. Perceived freedom in leisure and physical co-ordination ability: impact on out-of-school activity participation and life satisfaction. *Child: care, health and development, 33*, pp. 432-440.

Prellwitz, M. 2007. Playground accessibility and usability for children with disabilities. PhD thesis: Lulea University of Technology, Sweden.

Prellwitz, M. and Skar, L. 2007. Usability of playgrounds for children with different abilities. *Occupational Therapy International, 14* (3), pp. 144-155.

Prellwitz, M and Tamm, M. 1999. Attitudes of key persons to accessibility problems in playgrounds for children with restricted mobility: A study in a medium-sized municipality in northern Sweden. *Scandinavian Journal of Occupational Therapy, 6* (4), pp. 166-173.

Prellwitz, M. Tamm, M. and Lindqvist, R. 2001. Are playgrounds in Norrland (northern Sweden) accessible to children with restricted mobility? *Scandinavian Journal of Disability Research, 3*(1), pp. 56-68.

Putnam, T. and Newton, C. (Eds) 1990. *Household Choices*. London: Futures Publications.

Rapoport, A. 1995. A critical look at the concept "home"'. IN: Benjamin, D.N., Stea, D. and Saille, D. (eds) *The Home: Words, Interpretations, Meanings and Environments*. Aldershot: Avebury.

Richardson, P.K. 2002. The School as Social Context: Social Interaction. Patterns of Children with Physical Disabilities. *American Journal of Occupational Therapy, 56* (3), pp. 296–304.

Rigby, P. and Gaik, S. 2007. Stability of Playfulness Across Environmental Settings. A Pilot Study. *Physical and occupational Therapy in Paediatrics, 27* (1) pp. 27-43.

Rimmer, J.H., Riley, B., Wang, E., Rauworth, A. and Jurkowski, J. 2004. Physical activity participation among persons with disabilities: barriers and facilitators. *American Journal of Preventative Medicine, 26* (5), pp. 419-25.

Rubin, D.A., Wilson, K.S., Wierma, L.D., Weiss, J.W. and Rose, D.J. 2014. Rationale and design of active play @home: a parent-led physical activity program for children with and without disability, *BMC Pediatrics, 14* (1), pp.1-22.

Saelens, B.E. and Handy, S.L 2008. Built Environment Correlates of Walking: a review. *Medical Science Sports Exercise* 40 (Suppl 7) pp. S550 – 566.

Sandberg, A., Bjorck-Akesson, E. and Granlund, M. 2004. Play in retrospection: play experiences from childhood in adults with visual disability, motor disability and Asperger syndrome. *Scandinavian Journal of Disability Research, 6* (2), pp. 111-130.

Santer, J. Griffiths, C. and Goodall, D. 2007 *Free Play in Early Childhood*. London. Play England. Available from: http://www.playengland.org.uk/media/120426/free-play-in-early-childhood.pdf. [Accessed May 2015].

Schreuer, N., Sachs, D. and Rosenblum, S. 2014. Participation in leisure activities: Differences between children with and without physical disabilities. *Research in Developmental Disabilities*, 35 (1), pp. 223-233.

Shikako-Thomas, K., Shevell, M., Schmitz, N., Lach, L., Law, M., Poulin, C. and Majnemer, A. 2013. Determinants of participant in leisure activities among adolescents with cerebral palsy. *Research in developmental disabilities, 34*, pp. 2621-2634.

Shikako-Thomas, K., A. Majnemer, M. Law and Lach, L. 2008. Determinants of Participation in Leisure Activities in Children and Youth with Cerebral Palsy: Systematic Review. *Physical and Occupational Therapy in Pediatrics 28* (2), pp. 155–169.

Somerville, P. 1997. The social construction of home. *Journal of Architectural and Planning Research, 14* (1), pp. 226-245.

Spencer-Cavaliere, N. and Watkinson, E.J. 2010. Inclusion understood from the perspectives of children with disability. *Adapted Physical Activity Quarterly, 27* (4), pp. 275-93.

Sutton-Smith, B. 1997. *The Ambiguity of Play*. Cambridge, Massachusetts: Harvard University Press.

Taub, D.E. and Greer, K.R. 2000. Physical Activity as a Normalizing Experience for School-Age Children with Physical Disabilities. Implications for Legitimation of Social Identity and Enhancement of Social Ties. *Sport and Social Issues. 24* (4), pp. 395-414.

Taylor, A. F., Kuo, F. E. and Sullivan, W.C. 2001. Coping with ADD; The Surprising Connection to Green Play Settings. *Environment and Behaviour*, 33 (1).

Tomcheck, S. and Dunn, W. 2007. Sensory processing in children with and without autism: A comparative study using the Short Sensory Profile. *American Journal of Occupational Therapy, 61 (2)*, pp. 190-200.

Tonkin, B. L., Ogilvie, B. D., Greenwood, S.A., Law, M. C. and Anaby, D.R. 2014. The participation of children and youth with disabilities in activities outside of school: A scoping review. *The Canadian Journal of Occupational Therapy*. Available from: http://www.readperiodicals.com/201410/3559346221.html [Accessed August 30th 2015].

Tuan, Y. 1978. Children and the Natural Environment, *IN*: Altman, I. and Wohwill, J. (eds) *Children and the Environment*. New York: Plenum Press.

UK Government, 1995. *Disability Discrimination Act 1995*. Available from: Legislation.gov.uk. N.p., 1995 [Accessed 26th August 2015]

UNICEF. 2008. *Monitoring disability in developing countries: results from the multiple cluster survey*. New York, United Nations Children's Fund and University of Wisconsin, 2008. Available from: http://www.crin.org/resources/infodetail.asp?id=19377. [Accessed 23rd July 2015].

United Nations General Assembly 1959. *Declaration of the Rights of the Child* G.A. res. 1386 (XIV), 14 U.N. GAOR Supp. (No. 16) at 19, U.N. Doc. A/4354 (1959).

United Nations High Commissioner for Human Rights 1989. *UN Convention on the Rights of the Child* (UNCRC). Geneva: Office of the United Nations High Commissioner for Human Rights.

UN General Assembly. 2007. Convention on the Rights of Persons with Disabilities. Genova: United Nations

UN Committee on the Rights of the Child (CRC), General comment No. 9: The rights of children with disabilities. 2007. Available from: http://www.refworld.org/docid/461b93f72.html [Accessed 5th September 2015].

United Nations High Commissioner for Human Rights 2013. *General Comment 17*. The right of the child to rest, leisure, play, recreational activities, cultural life and the arts (Article 31). Geneva: United Nations

Valentine, G. and Holloway, S.L. (eds.) 2000. Children's Geographies; playing, living, learning. London: Routledge.

Victor, L. 2008. Systematic reviewing. Social *Research Update 54*. Available from: http://sru.soc.surrey.ac.uk/SRU54.pdf [Accessed 2nd July 2015].

Webb, R. 2003. *Public play provision for children with disabilities*. Dublin: National Disability Authority.

Wetherby, A.M. and Woods, J. 2006. Early social interaction project for children with autism spectrum disorders beginning the second life: a preliminary study. *Topics in Early Childhood Special Education, 26* (2), pp. 67-82.

WHO. 2012. *Early Childhood Development and Disability: A discussion paper*. Geneva: World Health Organization Press.

WHO, World Bank. 2012. *World report on disability*. Geneva, World Health OrganizationAvailable from http://www.who.int/disabilities/world_report/2011/en/index.html [Accessed 21st July 2015].

WHO. 2002. Towards a Common Language for Functioning, Disability and Health ICF. Geneva, World Health Organization. Available from: http://www.who.int/classifications/icf/en/ [Accessed 19th August 2015].

WHO. 2002. *International Classification of Function, Disability and Health (ICF)*. Geneva, World Health Organization. Available from: http://www.who.int/classifications/icf/en/ [Accessed 10th August 2015].

WHO. 2007. ICF-CY, International Classification of Functioning, Disability, and Health: Children & Youth version. Geneva: World Health Organization.

Woolley, H. 2013. Now Being Social: The Barrier of Designing Outdoor Play Spaces for Disabled Children. *Children and Society*, 27, pp. 448-458.

Bei Fragen zur Produktsicherheit wenden Sie sich bitte an:
If you have any questions regarding product safety,
please contact:

Walter de Gruyter GmbH
Genthiner Straße 13
10785 Berlin
productsafety@degruyterbrill.com